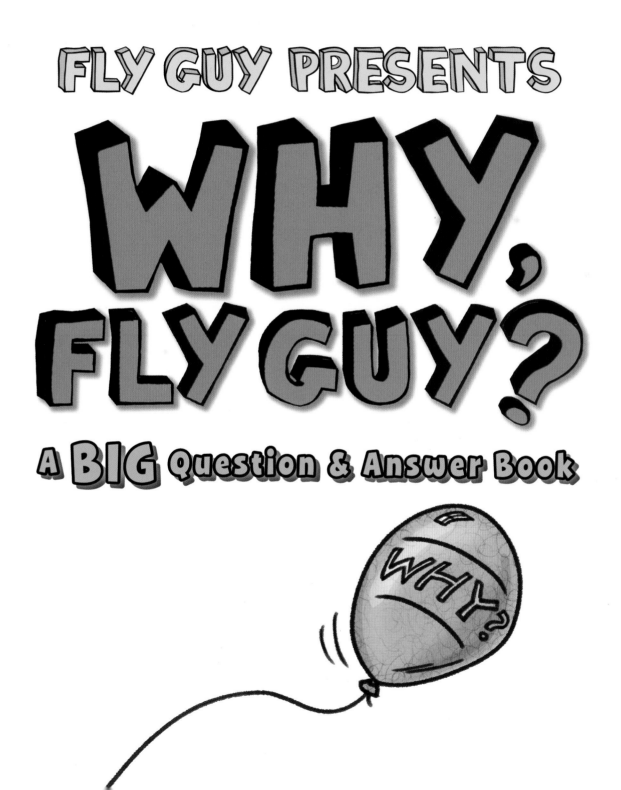

FLY GUY PRESENTS

WHY, FLY GUY?

A BIG Question & Answer Book

For Ella, Noah, Anastazia, and Vytas—T.A.

Thank you to the following for their contributions to this book:
AnnMarie Anderson, Ashley Pagnotta at the American Museum of Natural History, The Elephant Sanctuary in Tennessee,
Dr. Megan Griffiths in the Department of Biological Sciences at Kent State University, Meteorologist Scott Collis,
Narges Farahi, M.D., and Richard Baker at the American Museum of Natural History.

Library of Congress Cataloging-in-Publication Data
Names: Arnold, Tedd, author, illustrator. | Arnold, Tedd. Fly Guy presents—
Title: Why, Fly Guy? / by Tedd Arnold.
Description: New York, NY : Scholastic Inc., 2017. | Series: Fly Guy presents |
Includes index. | Audience: Ages 4–8. | Audience: K to grade 3.
Identifiers: LCCN 2016054931 | ISBN 9781338053180 (paper over board)
Subjects: LCSH: Children's questions and answers. | Science—Juvenile literature.
Classification: LCC Q163 .A7855 2017 | DDC 031—
dc23 LC record available at https://lccn.loc.gov/2016054931

ISBN 978-1-338-05318-0

12 11 10 9 8 7 6 5 4 3 2 1   17 18 19 20 21

Printed in China 38
First printing, September 2017

Book design by Baily Crawford

FLY GUY PRESENTS

WHY, FLY GUY?

A BIG Question & Answer Book

Tedd Arnold

Scholastic Inc.

A boy had a pet fly named Fly Guy. Fly Guy could say the boy's name—

Buzz had a lot of questions. Luckily, he and Fly Guy were about to get some answers. . . .

·TABLE OF CONTENTS·

THE BUZZ ON BUZZ!

THE BUZZ ON BEES AND OTHER ANIMALS

THE BUZZ ON PLANTS AND NATURE

THE BUZZ ON OTHER COOL STUFF

The Buzz on BUZZ!

I can't wait to read all about the human body!

Why do my feet smell?

Bacteria are tiny creatures that live on the skin all over your body. Bacteria feed on your sweat, creating a stinky odor. The smell of sweat is worst on your feet because shoes trap the stink. If you wear the same shoes every day, your shoes don't have a chance to air out. And that makes stinky feet even smellier!

Why do bacteria live on me?

Bacteria live everywhere— on people, pets, dirt, air, water, and even clouds! To stay alive, bacteria need nutrients from their environment. Bacteria are just one type of germ. All bacteria are germs, but not all germs are bacteria! Some bacteria are good for you, and others can be bad (or just stinky). Germs are the same—some are good, but others can make you sick.

bacteria

Why does my heart beat?

Your heart is a muscle. It works like a pump. Every time your heart squeezes, it pushes blood through your arteries. Your blood brings oxygen to different parts of your body.

Your muscles need oxygen to move. When you exercise, your muscles move a lot. So your body needs more oxygen! That's why your heart beats faster when you run, swim, or play hard. It's moving more blood through your arteries.

model of a human heart

Why do I bruise?

Blood flows through your body in blood vessels. When part of your body is bumped or banged, tiny blood vessels called capillaries sometimes break. Blood spills out of the capillaries and gathers right under your skin. This causes a bruise. But your body heals itself: The bruise will change color as your body slowly absorbs the blood again.

13

Why do my teeth fall out?

Your teeth fall out to make room for more teeth! Kids have fewer teeth than adults because you have smaller heads and mouths than adults.

X-ray of a child's mouth

Little kids have 20 primary teeth. Primary teeth are also called "milk teeth" or "baby teeth." As you grow, bigger teeth push these smaller teeth up and out.

Most adults have 32 teeth. If you lose an adult tooth, a new one won't replace it!

Why do I have to brush my teeth?

After you eat, some food is left behind. Bacteria turn the leftover food into acid. If you don't clean the acid off, it burns through the tough, thin enamel that coats your teeth. Sometimes this leads to a cavity, which is a hole in your tooth. Cavities can make your teeth hurt. Bacteria in your mouth can also cause bad breath. Yuck! Brush twice a day to keep your mouth and teeth healthy and your breath fresh-smelling.

Sharks don't have to brush their teeth. It is normal for their teeth to fall out and grow back over and over.

IF FLY GUY COULD TALK...

Hi, there!

You know, after a long day of dumpster diving...

...sidewalk licking...

...and roadkill snacks...

...it actually feels good to brush my teeth!

17

Brush an egg!

You will need:

- a white, hard-boiled egg (Ask an adult to help with this part!)

- a mason jar, pint glass, mug, or small bowl

- 12-24 ounces dark grape juice

- a toothbrush

- toothpaste

What to do:

1. Look at the color of the egg. Now place it in the jar.

2. Pour enough grape juice into the jar to cover the egg completely.

3. Let the egg sit for 5 hours.

4. Remove and dry the egg. What color is it now?

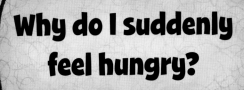

5. Put some toothpaste on the toothbrush.

6. Brush the egg. See what happens!

Note: Do NOT eat the egg you used in this project.

Why do I suddenly feel hungry?

Why, Fly Guy?

The shell of a hard-boiled egg is a lot like a tooth. The grape juice is left behind on the egg, but brushing the egg with toothpaste makes it clean again!

Why do my ears make wax?

Special sweat glands in your ears make sticky earwax. This shiny stuff keeps your ears clean and healthy. It traps dust and germs to keep them from getting inside your body.

Earwax can be dry and white or wet and yellowish brown.

NAZZ-TEE!

What?

Later, with the doctor
Sometimes, too much earwax can plug up your hearing.

What?

21

Why do my eyes get crusty when I sleep?

When you are awake, tears and mucus push oil, dust, dead skin, and other gunk out of your eyes each time you blink. But when your eyes are closed, this gunk gathers in the corners and dries out. When you open your eyes in the morning, the corners are crusty.

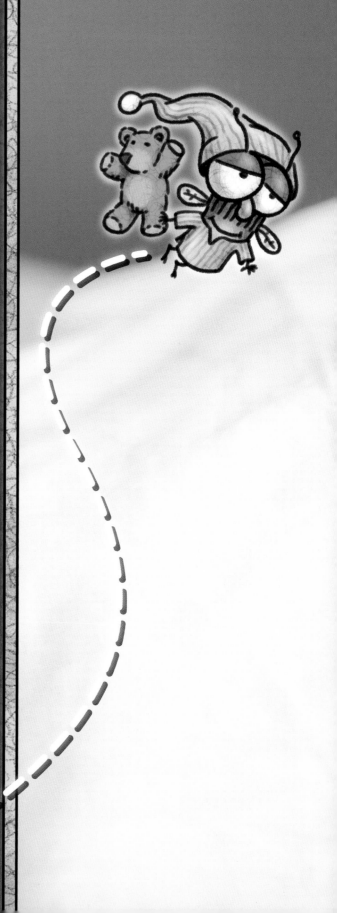

Why do tears taste salty?

Salt is everywhere in your body—in your blood, sweat, and even your tears! Salt helps keep everything in the body running smoothly.

Why do I sneeze?

You sneeze to keep stuff out of your body. When dust, dirt, and germs get in your nose, your brain tells your body to get rid of them. When you sneeze, air rushes out of your lungs. The air flies out of your nose and mouth, taking the dust and germs with it!

I never hear Fly Guy sneeze. I wonder why?

SNEEZZZ?

Why does my nose run?

Every nose makes thick, gooey mucus. It traps dust, dirt, and germs in your nose before they get inside your body. Usually, mucus drips down your throat and is swallowed. But sometimes your nose makes more mucus than usual, and it dribbles out. This can happen when you are sick, when it is cold outside, or when you cry.

IF FLY GUY COULD TALK...

Why don't I sneeze? Good question.

I drew a picture of my insides.

RADAR EYEZ

WINGZ

GUTZ

FEETZ

You can see, I have lots of guts but no lungs. No lungs means no sneezing.

WINGZ

GUTZ

I breathe through these small side holes called spiracles.

WINGZ

GUTZ

This nose thingie is actually called a proboscis. It's for eating, not sneezing. I'm a complicated guy.

WINGZ

GU

Why do I have to wash my hands?

Germs can be anywhere. Many germs are bad. Your hands touch things that may have germs. Then your hands might touch your mouth or your food. If a germ gets inside your body, it can make you sick. But there's one easy way to kill germs: with soap and water!

This germ causes strep throat!

How to wash your hands:

1. Wet your hands.

2. Add soap and scrub for 20 seconds.*

> I sing "Happy Birthday" twice.

3. Rinse with water.

4. Dry your hands.

*Be sure to wash your fingertips, nails, and between your fingers.

27

Why do I eat?

Your body needs energy to grow, run, jump, and play! You eat because food gives you energy. Food also has **nutrients** and **vitamins** that keep your body healthy and strong.

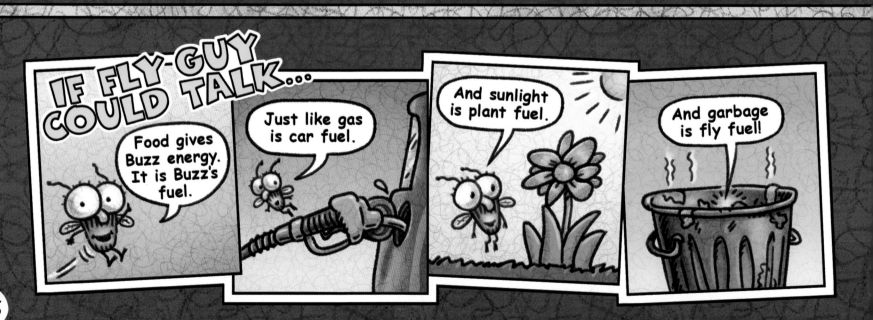

Why do I poop?

After your food is broken into tiny pieces (a process called digestion), a lot of it enters your blood. That is where it gives your body energy. But some food doesn't turn into energy. The extra fiber and cells from the food mix with mucus in your body. Together, this leftover stuff comes out as poop!

Why do I burp?

When you eat or drink, you swallow extra air along with your sandwich or juice. Air is made of gases like nitrogen and oxygen. When there is too much gas in your stomach, it gets pushed back up—burp!

Fizzy drinks make you burp more than water, milk, or juice. This is because a gas called carbon dioxide was added to them. More gas means more burps!

MUNCH CRUNCH SLURP

GOBBLE CRUNCH SLORP

BURP

Sometimes, when Fly Guy enjoys his dinner, it kinda ruins mine.

GULP LICK MUNCH

Why do I fart?

Sometimes the extra air you swallow eating and drinking doesn't go back up in a burp. Instead, it goes out the back end as a fart! Bacteria in your stomach breaks down food to make gas. There are also chemicals in your stomach that make more gas. Extra gas gets pushed out in farts.

Why do I hiccup?

Hic Hic Hic

The **diaphragm** is a muscle below your lungs. When you take a breath, it pushes down as your lungs fill with air. But sometimes the diaphragm starts to twitch on its own. Each time it twitches, you breathe in quickly. When this happens, air hits your voice box, and you make a "hic" sound.

No one knows exactly why this happens. Some people get hiccups when they eat too much or eat too quickly. Others get hiccups when they are scared, nervous, or excited. Most hiccups go away in a few minutes.

32

Next time you get the hiccups, try getting rid of them using one of these tricks!

- Hold a pencil horizontally between your teeth while you drink water from a glass.

- Hold a paper bag over your mouth and nose. Breathe in and out for 1 minute.

- Hold your breath and count to 10.

- Drink from the wrong side of the glass.

- Place a teaspoon of sugar on the back of your tongue and swallow it.

- Get someone to scare you!

Hic

Hic

Why do I yawn?

No one really knows! Some scientists think people yawn when they need to breathe in more air. Other scientists think a yawn sends a message to other people that you are bored or tired. Yawning might even help keep the brain cool so that it doesn't get too hot!

WARNING: Yawning is contagious! If you yawn, people who see you do it might also yawn.

Why do I sleep?

No one knows for sure exactly why people sleep, but it is as important as eating and drinking! Your muscles grow slowly over time, and the body needs sleep for this to happen. If any part of your body is sick or hurt, it can rest and heal while you sleep. Sleep is also good for your brain. Sleep helps make it easier for you to learn and do different things when you're awake.

I wonder what Fly Guy dreams about. He looks so peaceful.

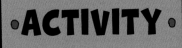

Make a dream journal!

Everyone dreams! Dreams can help you learn and remember things.

Most people remember less than 5% of their dreams after they wake up!

Keep a journal of your dreams for one week. Each morning, write down or draw a picture of your dream.

At the end of the week, look back at your journal. Did your dreams change each day? Or did you have the same dream again and again?

The Buzz on Bees and Other Animals

Why do bees make honey?

Honeybees eat nectar from flowers. They turn some of this nectar into honey. They store the honey in their beehive. When it gets cold and snowy in the winter, there aren't as many flowers. This is when honeybees eat the honey they stored during the warmer months. It's their food!

honey

40

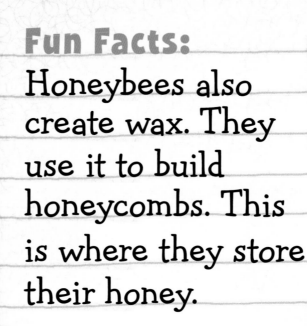
honeybee

Fun Facts:

Honeybees also create wax. They use it to build honeycombs. This is where they store their honey.

honeycomb

Honeycombs are always hexagon-shaped.

1
6   2
hexagon
5   3
4

Bumblebees don't make as much honey as honeybees. People don't eat bumblebee honey.

bumblebee

Why do fireflies light up?

abdomen

Fireflies have special chemicals in their abdomens. When the chemicals meet oxygen in their bodies, the fireflies' abdomens light up. This is called bioluminescence. Fireflies use their lights to help find other fireflies. They also light up to warn animals not to eat them—the glowing chemicals taste bad!

Other creatures use bioluminescence, too!

cuttlefish

jellyfish

squid

There are around 2,000 different types of fireflies, and each type uses a different pattern of lights.

Fireflies, also called lightning bugs, aren't flies or bugs. They are beetles!

Fly Guy, I need to use your jar.

A few minutes later...

Look! I caught a firefly.

I have to go tell Mom and Dad!

Soon, Buzz hurried back with Mom and Dad.

Hey, where's my firefly?

Who knowzz?

Why do flies have compound eyes?

Each of your eyes has one lens. But houseflies have compound eyes. Each compound eye has thousands of lenses, so flies can see in almost every direction. That means they don't have to turn their heads to see above, below, or behind them.

Compound eyes are great at detecting movement! If something gets close, a fly can plan an escape route in less than one hundredth of a second.

what fly eyes see

Why do flies buzz?

Houseflies make a buzzing sound when they fly. This sound is made by the beating of their two wings.

A fly's wings move up and down about 200 times in one second!

Flies are one of the fastest insects!

Why do cats get stuck in trees?

Cats get stuck in trees because their claws curve in. This makes it impossible for a cat to climb back down headfirst. Most cats can jump down or climb down tailfirst. But many are too scared to figure this out. Instead, they stay put and wait to be rescued.

If a cat does fall, it will almost always twist around so that it lands on its feet.

It is easy for me to go up and down a tree! House cats can climb <u>up</u> a tree...

...but they can't climb <u>down</u>.

Even if they can land on their feet, being up high in a tree can be scary to a cat.

So, please leave the tree climbing to us experts.

Just don't tell Fluffy his cat tree isn't real.

Only two cats can climb down trees headfirst:

- The margay is a rare cat found in the rain forests of Mexico, Central America, and South America.

margay

- The clouded leopard lives in the forests of Southeast Asia.

clouded leopard

47

Why do skunks stink?

Skunks don't always smell bad. But if another animal comes close and a skunk gets scared, it will squirt out an oily spray from glands under its tail. This spray smells awful! The smell usually scares away any animal that was thinking of eating the skunk for lunch.

Skunks have good aim. They can spray an animal or a person from 10 feet away!

Why do some animals sleep all winter?

In the winter, it is harder for some animals to find food. So they hibernate, or go into a deep sleep, instead of staying awake. While hibernating, the animals' bodies use up stored body fat. Their body temperature drops, their breathing slows, and they are very still. It is hard to wake most hibernating animals.

DO NOT DISTURB!

hibernating dormouse

Bears:

Bears hibernate differently from other animals. Black bears and brown bears use up stored body fat (just like other hibernators). But their body temperature only drops a little bit. Also, hibernating bears can be woken very easily.

hibernating black bears

51

Why don't polar bears get cold?

Polar bears are different from other bears. They live in a cold climate, but they don't hibernate. Instead, they spend the winter eating. Their bodies have a special ability to turn food into heat energy, which keeps them warm. Polar bears also have a thick layer of fat called blubber. Their fat is topped with a coat of fur that helps them stay toasty warm!

POLAR BRRRZZ!

Why do birds have feathers?

Different birds have feathers for different reasons. The reason changes from bird to bird! Some birds' feathers help them eat, hear, swim, fly, stay clean, stay dry, build nests, or hide from other animals.

All birds have feathers to help them stay warm. Feathers trap air close to the bird's body. A bird fluffs its feathers so the feathers trap more air and keep the bird warmer.

Feathers also help birds fly. Flight feathers have a special shape. One half is wide and the other is narrow, like the wing of an airplane. This shape helps create lift, which is the force that keeps the bird in the air.

Dinosaurs are related to birds. Some even had feathers!

velociraptor

TICKLZZZ?

Stop it, Fly Guy!

Make feather and blubber mittens!

You will need:

- four quart-sized plastic bags

- 20-30 cotton balls

- duct tape

- 1 cup vegetable shortening

- a bowl

- ice cubes

What to do:

1. Fill one plastic bag with the cotton balls. Place a second plastic bag inside the first. Seal the top of the first bag to the top of the second bag with tape around the outside of each bag, leaving an opening in the middle. This should create a plastic bag mitten with an inner lining of cotton balls. You should be able to place your hand inside so that the cotton balls surround your hand.

2. Fill one plastic bag with the vegetable shortening. Place a second plastic bag inside the first. Seal the top of the first bag to the top of the second bag, just like you did before. This should create a plastic bag mitten with an inner lining of shortening.

3. Fill the bowl with ice cubes.

4. Place your bare hand in the bowl of ice. How does it feel?

5. Now place your hand in the mitten filled with cotton balls. Then put it in the bowl of ice. How does it feel? Do the same thing with the mitten filled with shortening.

Why, Fly Guy?

In the feather mitten, the cotton balls act like fluffed-up feathers on a bird. They trap air and keep your hand warm, just like the feathers on a bird keep its body warm. In the blubber mitten, the shortening acts like the layer of blubber on a polar bear. It keeps your hand warm, just like the blubber on a polar bear keeps its body warm.

Why do birds fly in a "V" shape?

The feathers of the birds in front create air currents. The birds in the back hitch a ride on these currents! This helps the birds in the back of the flock fly faster and more easily. As they fly, the birds switch places to give the leaders a rest. This "V" shape is called an echelon.

58

When bicyclists ride in a pack, they do the same thing as birds! They call it "drafting" or "slipstreaming."

peloton

A group of bicycle riders is called a peloton.

Why do jellyfish sting?

Jellyfish sting to defend themselves. They also sting to catch their dinner. Each jellyfish tentacle is covered in tiny threads that shoot poison into the jellyfish's prey. The poison can make it hard for the other animal to move. This means the jellyfish can chow down!

ALIENZZ!

60

Jellyfish do kind of look like aliens! But they're not. And a group of jellyfish is called a bloom or a smack.

Why do sea stars' arms grow back?

Sea stars are special creatures. They can regenerate, or grow, new limbs. That's because each sea star arm contains all of the important parts the sea star needs to stay alive. It can take as long as a year for an arm to grow back after it breaks off.

Some worms can regenerate their heads and bodies, too!

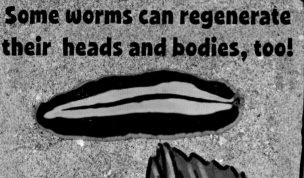
green anole lizard

The green anole lizard can regrow a lost tail.

Why do dolphins jump out of the water?

FUNZIE!

Scientists aren't sure why dolphins jump. Dolphins might jump so they can get a better look at the world around them as they search for food. Or they might jump to communicate with other dolphins. Another idea is that dolphins jump because they like it! Dolphins are friendly and, like many animals, they enjoy playing. Have you ever jumped just for fun?

Why do turtles have shells?

A turtle's shell acts like a knight's armor. It is made of bone, so it's very hard! It protects the turtle's body and keeps it safe from other animals that might want to harm it. Some turtles can pull their heads, necks, arms, and legs inside their shells for extra protection. But other turtles—like sea turtles—can't.

Sea turtle shells are covered with an extra layer of leathery skin!

I am Sir Buzz.

I fear nothing.

My armor is—

BOOZZ!

HA HA HA!

65

Why do whales have blowholes?

A whale's blowhole is its nose. It lets the whale breathe. Some people think whales blow seawater out of their blowholes. But this isn't true. When a whale breathes warm air out, it meets cold air above the water and changes to steam. This steam is full of whale mucus, not water.

Scientists collect and study whale snot using special flying robots called SnotBots.

SnotBot

SnotBot near whale

blowhole

Why do elephants have trunks?

An elephant's trunk is a combination of its top lip and its nose. It is not used for eating or drinking. Elephants use their trunks to breathe, smell, touch, grab, and make sounds.

The trunk is very strong. It can lift over 750 pounds! That's the weight of a small grizzly bear. And the trunk contains more than 40,000 muscles. (The human body only has 639!)

Fun Facts:

An elephant trunk is the world's longest nose!

An elephant uses its trunk like a snorkel to help it breathe while underwater!

elephant using its trunk as a snorkel

boy snorkeling

Elephants can suck water into their trunks and blow it out.

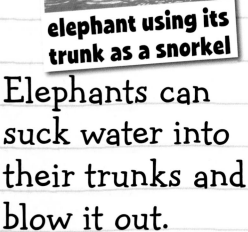

Splash!

If there were an award for Most Unique Body Part, elephants would win it!

MOST UNIQUE BODY PART

69

Fun Fact:

An elephant's trunk is like a person's hand. The elephant can use its trunk to lift and touch things.

African elephants have two "fingers."

Asian elephants have one "finger."

Use your hand like an elephant's trunk!

Pretend your hand is an elephant's trunk. Try picking up different things using two fingers, like an African elephant. Then try it with just one finger, like an Asian elephant. It isn't easy!

Some things to try:
- A pencil
- A paper clip
- A banana
- An apple
- An empty paper cup
- A spoon

71

Why can't I see the air?

When we see objects, what we are actually seeing is light reflecting off the object and into our eyes. Air is made of gases such as oxygen and nitrogen. These gases do not block the light, so the light passes directly through the air.

But solid objects, like a fly, do block the light. So the light reflects off the objects back into our eyes. That's why you can see a fly, but you can't see the air around it.

Light comes from a light source, like the Sun, then it bounces off Fly Guy and goes into my eyes.

Why do plants need water?

Plants need energy to grow. People eat food to get energy, but plants create their own food. This is called photosynthesis (fo-to-SIN-the-sis). Plants create their food from sunlight, carbon dioxide in the air, and water.

SUNLIGHT

OXYGEN

LEAVES

WATER

CARBON DIOXIDE

STEM

ROOTS

NUTRIENTS

Water carries nutrients out of the soil and up into the plant's leaves. In most plants, photosynthesis happens in the leaves.

Why do potatoes grow underground?

Potato plants grow aboveground, just like other vegetables. But the tasty part grows under the soil! About four weeks after it is planted, a potato plant's aboveground stem and leaves stop growing. But the short underground stems continue to get bigger.

The potato is the most popular vegetable in the United States.

FRIES

KETCHUP

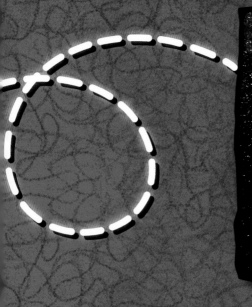

Potatoes are tuber plants. The potato is called a "stem tuber." In this plant, the tuber is the short, thick, mostly underground stem that holds nutrients and has buds that grow into new plant shoots.

Have you ever seen an old potato with small stems growing out of it? If you planted your old potato, those small stems would grow into a new potato plant!

an old potato

The potato was the first vegetable grown in space!

Why do leaves change color?

Most plants contain a chemical called chlorophyll. It helps them absorb the energy in sunlight to make food. Chlorophyll is also what makes leaves look green. In the fall, leaves stop making food because there is less sunlight. The chlorophyll breaks down. This is why the leaves lose their green color. When the chlorophyll is gone, the leaves change to yellow, orange, brown, red, or purple.

Many of these colors were there all along, but the bright green chlorophyll was covering them up!

Why do seashells sound like the sea?

It might sound like you can hear waves crashing on the beach inside a seashell, but it's not the sea that you're hearing. When you hold a shell close to your ear, the background noise around you gets trapped inside. The sound waves bounce off the shell's smooth, hard inside and echo loudly in your ear.

Also, try it with a cup.

Why does it rain?

When the Sun warms water in lakes, rivers, and oceans on Earth, the water turns from a liquid to a gas. Then it rises into the air, forming clouds. As the air gets cooler, the water changes from a gas back to a liquid or a solid. It can fall to Earth as rain, hail, or snow. This is called the water cycle.

CLOUDS

SUN

WATER CYCLE

PRECIPITATION

EVAPORATION

Raindrops aren't shaped like tears. As a raindrop falls, the top remains curved while the bottom flattens out like the top of a hamburger bun.

Why does thunder follow lightning?

Lightning is a giant electric spark. It is hotter than the Sun. When lightning strikes, the air gets hot so quickly that it makes sound waves vibrate. This creates a boom of thunder.

You often don't hear thunder until a few seconds after lightning. This is because sound moves slower than light. The closer you are to the lightning, the sooner you'll hear the thunder.

Why do tornadoes form?

A funnel cloud can form when a powerful thunderstorm meets winds that change direction as they move up into the sky. If the funnel cloud touches the ground, it is called a tornado. If a funnel cloud touches water, it is called a waterspout.

If you hear a tornado siren, seek shelter right away!

Make a tornado in a jar!

You will need:

- a mason jar with a lid
- water
- about 2 tablespoons dishwashing detergent
- glitter (optional)

What to do:

1. Add water to the jar until it is three-quarters of the way full.

2. Squirt the dishwashing detergent into the jar.

3. Add glitter.

4. Screw on the cap tightly.

5. Spin the jar in a spiral motion for about 30 seconds.* Watch what happens!

*Tip: If the liquid is too cloudy, let the jar sit for 10–15 minutes. Then try again.

Why, Fly Guy?

When you spin the jar, you create a spinning column of water—your very own funnel cloud! This is the same thing that happens when a powerful thunderstorm meets winds that change direction.

Why do astronauts float in space?

Astronauts aren't floating—they're falling! Gravity is the force that pulls something toward Earth's center. It's the reason this book will fall to the ground if you drop it. Astronauts feel gravity even when they are inside the International Space Station. But the space station is moving around Earth in an orbit—a regular, repeating path. As the space station moves, it's actually falling around the Earth in its orbit. That means the astronauts inside it are falling, too! Since the astronauts and the space station are falling around the Earth at the same speed, it looks like the astronauts are floating.

Why does the Sun rise and set?

Earth spins around completely once each day, which is called rotation. As Earth spins, the Sun shines on different parts of the planet. When the part of Earth where you are rotates toward the Sun at the beginning of the day, you begin to see its light. It looks as if the Sun is rising. As Earth rotates away from the Sun at the end of your day, its light fades. It looks as if the Sun is setting. But it's really Earth that is moving, not the Sun!

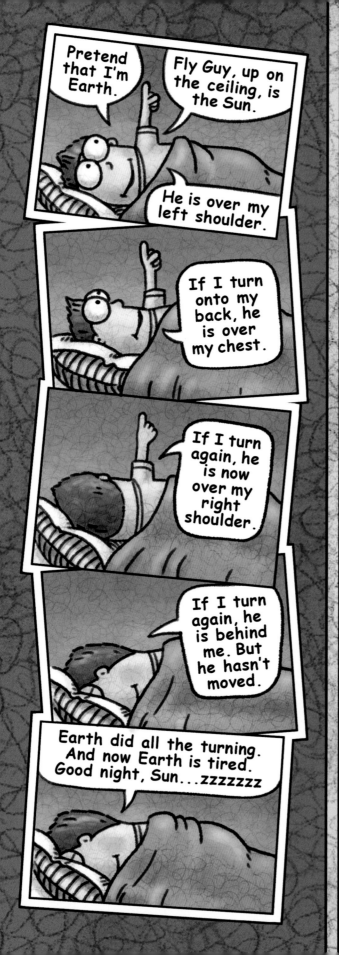

Why does the Moon only come out at night?

It doesn't! The Moon reflects the bright light of the Sun. (It doesn't make any of its own light.) Sometimes the Moon is overhead, but the Sun is so bright we cannot see it. It's easiest to see the Moon at night because the sky is dark.

Why does the Moon change shape?

The Moon doesn't change shape. It just looks like it does because we're seeing it from Earth! As the Moon moves around Earth, different parts of it are lit up by the Sun. The amount of Moon we see depends on where the Moon is in its 28-day loop around the Earth.

28-day loop

From our viewpoint on Earth, the Moon has 8 different shapes, called phases.

The Sun

| New | Waxing Crescent | First Quarter | Waxing Gibbous | Full | Waning Gibbous | Third Quarter | Waning Crescent |

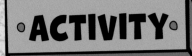

Play with your food!

Learn the order and names of the eight key phases of the Moon using cookies.

You will need:

- 1 blank piece of paper

- markers or crayons

- eight round sandwich cookies

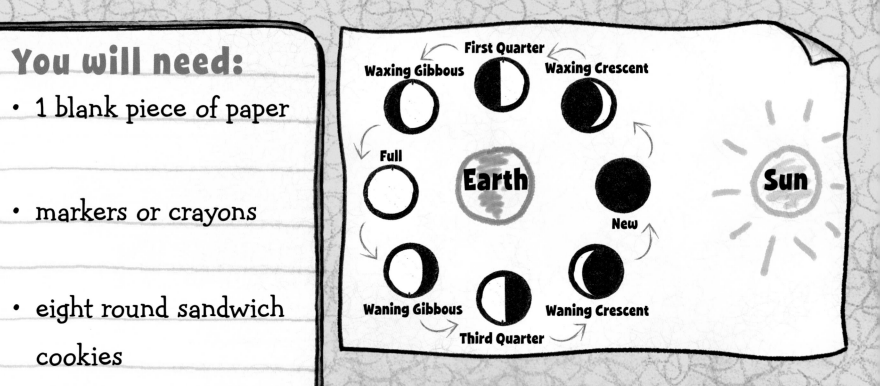

What to do:

Draw Earth in the center of the paper. Draw the Sun on the far right. Then use the cookies to illustrate and label the phases of the Moon.

1. New Moon
   (no cream)

2. Waxing crescent
   (sliver of cream on
   right side of cookie)

3. First quarter
   (cream on right
   half of cookie)

4. Waxing gibbous
   (cream fills right
   half of cookie and
   part of the left half
   as well)

5. Full Moon
   (all cream)

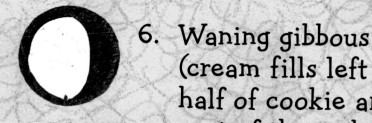

6. Waning gibbous
   (cream fills left
   half of cookie and
   part of the right
   half as well)

7. Third quarter
   (cream on left half
   of cookie)

8. Waning crescent
   (sliver of cream on
   left side of cookie)

9. Eat up!

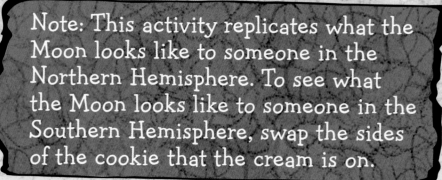

Note: This activity replicates what the
Moon looks like to someone in the
Northern Hemisphere. To see what
the Moon looks like to someone in the
Southern Hemisphere, swap the sides
of the cookie that the cream is on.

Why does soap make bubbles?

When you wash your hands, soap mixes with water. This mixture forms a thin film of soapy water. The film catches and holds pockets of air, creating bubbles.

Hey, Fly Guy! Want to get inside of a bubble?

YEZZ!

Okay, fly in front of my mouth, and I will blow you in.

Ready? Go!

WOOSH

It worked!

SWEETZZ!

Why does glue stick?

When you place one solid surface against another, tiny gaps between the two keep them from sticking together. Because glue is a liquid, it fills in these gaps. Once the glue hardens and dries, it creates a strong bond between the two surfaces.

Have you ever gotten sap from a pine tree or a pinecone on your hands or clothes? It's very sticky! That's because sap is a natural glue.

sap from pine tree

Make glue from milk!

YOU WILL NEED AN ADULT'S HELP FOR THIS PROJECT!

You will need:

- ½ cup milk

- 2 teaspoons distilled white vinegar

- ¼ teaspoon baking soda

- a small pot

- a sieve

- a small mixing bowl

What to do:

1. Pour the milk into a small pot. Ask an adult to help heat the milk slowly while stirring it. Remove from the heat when it is hot but not yet boiling.

2. Add the vinegar. Stir until the mixture gets lumpy.

3. With an adult's help, pour the hot liquid through a sieve. Save the lumps. Rinse them with cold water (still in the sieve).

4. Place the lumps in a small mixing bowl. Add the baking soda.

5. Slowly add ½ teaspoon water. Stir until the mixture is a thick paste. Add more water for a thinner paste.

6. You've got glue! Try using it to paste paper together. Then compare it to glue from the store. What do you notice?

Why, Fly Guy?

Milk is made of some of the same things as tree sap and other natural glues. Adding the vinegar to the milk helps separate the sticky substance from the milk, so you can use it to make natural glue!

Why do balloons float?

Different gases have different weights. The air around us is made mostly of two gases—nitrogen and oxygen. You can blow air into balloons to fill them up. Those balloons do not float because the air inside them matches the outside air. But if you fill balloons with helium, a gas that is lighter than nitrogen and oxygen, they will rise up higher than the air around them.

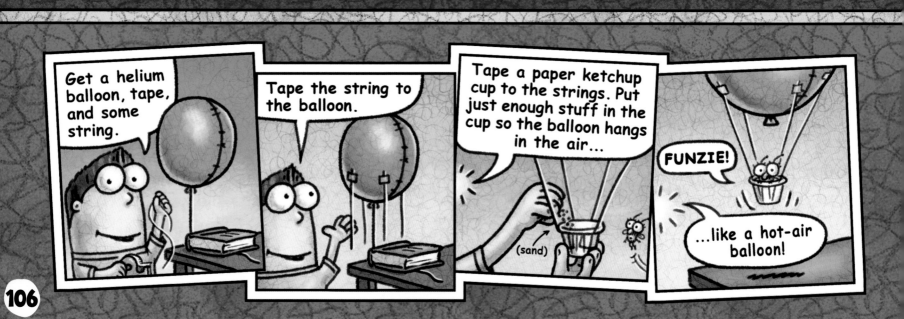

Get a helium balloon, tape, and some string.

Tape the string to the balloon.

Tape a paper ketchup cup to the strings. Put just enough stuff in the cup so the balloon hangs in the air...

(sand)

FUNZIE!

...like a hot-air balloon!

Why do balloons go "pop!" when they break?

Latex is a stretchy rubber. When a latex balloon is filled, the latex stretches out and the balloon gets bigger. The air inside the balloon puts pressure on the stretched-out latex. If you poke a hole in the balloon, the air inside rushes out with a loud "pop!" sound, and the latex snaps back to its original size.

Fun Fact:

Some balloons are made from Mylar, a foil-like plastic. If you poke a hole in a Mylar balloon, the air seeps out slowly. There is no "pop!"

Why is the Statue of Liberty green?

The Statue of Liberty is made from copper, the same metal as pennies. When the statue was first built in 1886, it was a brown-bronze color, just like a penny.

By 1920, oxygen and nitrogen gases in the air created a greenish-blue coating on the statue's copper surface. This is something that happens naturally to copper when it is left out in the air, wind, rain, and sun.

The Statue of Liberty, as designed by Frédéric Auguste Bartholdi (1884).

Why don't we clean the statue so it goes back to its original color?

The greenish-blue coating actually protects the Statue of Liberty! Without it, the air, wind, rain, and sun would eat away at the copper and make it break down even more than it has already.

Why don't pennies turn green, too?

A penny is coated in copper. If you left a penny outside in the air, wind, rain, and sun long enough, it would turn green! But most pennies ride around in your pockets. Fabric from your shirt or pants rubs against the penny and polishes it. So most pennies stay a brown-bronze color.

Our penny is officially called a "cent."

Why are tires filled with air?

Tires are made of rubber. Solid rubber tires are heavy. Air is lighter than solid rubber, so filling tires with air makes them lighter and easier to handle. Also, air is a good cushion. When you ride over a bump, an air-filled tire changes shape a bit so you don't feel the jolt. The air makes your ride more comfortable.

Why are wheels round?

Round wheels roll most easily. This is because the distance across a circle is the same no matter which way it turns. When you ride in a car that's sitting on four circles or on a bicycle that's sitting on two, your height doesn't change as you ride. Instead, the wheels turn smoothly and you stay level, with no jolts up and down.

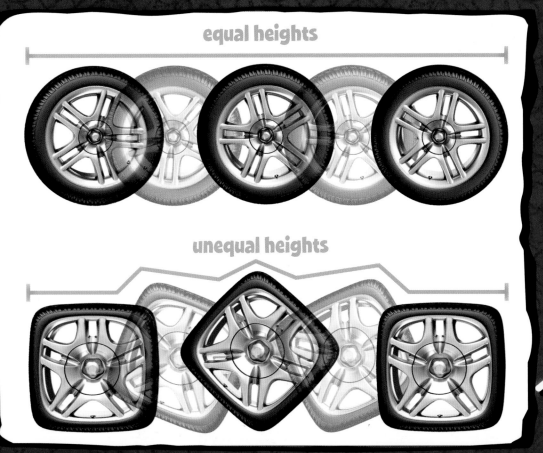

equal heights

unequal heights

Why does garbage smell?

Bacteria love to eat garbage. They break it down into smaller and smaller pieces. This is called decomposition. The small bits left behind are very stinky. When bacteria eat proteins like meat, dairy, fish, and eggs, nitrogen and sulfur form. These are super-smelly gases. That's why rotting meat smells worse than rotting fruit and vegetables.

Farts contain sulfur, too! That's why they stink.

IF FLY GUY COULD TALK...

Flies have a nose for garbage.

Actually, us flies smell through our antennae. If the wind is right, flies can smell a big pile of garbage from almost five miles away.

It might take several days for a little fly to travel that far.

But **WOW!** It is <u>so</u> worth it!

Why is the White House white?

The White House was built in 1800 from a type of rock called sandstone. The original builders painted the building to protect the sandstone from getting worn down. They probably chose white to match the color of the stone.

It takes 570 gallons of paint to cover the outside of the building!

For many years, people called the president's home "the white house." But the name didn't become official until 1901, when President Theodore Roosevelt added it to his stationery.

Why do stop signs have eight sides?

When states first started using street signs, it was decided that a sign's shape would show the danger level. Generally, signs for the most dangerous things had the most sides. A circle was used for railroad crossings because that shape was thought to be made up of many, many sides. The eight-sided octagon was chosen for the stop sign.

Diamonds were used for general warnings. Squares and rectangles were used for directions or other information. And triangles were used for yield signs.

Stop signs weren't always red! Early stop signs were yellow with black letters.

Make your own shaped signs!

Walk around your house looking for things that might be dangerous. Then make signs to warn others—just like street signs!

You will need:

- colored paper

- scissors

- crayons or markers

- tape

1. Choose your paper. Use different colored paper for different things. For example:

    - Use red for the most dangerous things.

    - Use yellow for less dangerous things.

    - Use green for informational signs.

2. Cut out shapes and write labels on them. Use different shapes for different things—just like street signs. Here are some examples:

- A red octagon near the stove might read: HOT!

- A yellow triangle near the stairs might read: WATCH YOUR STEP!

- A green square near the light switch might read: ON/OFF

3. Use tape to hang up your signs for the rest of your family to see.

BUZZ'S MESSY ROOM

"I can't believe how much I just learned, Fly Guy!" Buzz told his friend.

Fly Guy couldn't agree more. He felt like the smartest fly on Earth!

WIZZZE!

GLOSSARY

arteries: Tubes that carry blood from the heart to other parts of the body.

bacteria: One type of germ. Some bacteria are good for you while others can make you sick.

bioluminescence: Light produced by a living thing.

blood vessels: Tubes that carry blood through the body.

capillaries: The thinnest, smallest blood vessels.

carbon dioxide: A gas made of carbon and oxygen. It has no color or odor. (Carbon dioxide is not the same gas you put in your car.)

chlorophyll: The green substance in plants that uses light to make food from carbon dioxide and water.

contagious: Something that spreads to and affects other people.

decomposition: The process by which something rots or breaks down into smaller parts.

diaphragm: The muscle between your chest and abdomen.

digestion: The process by which food in the stomach and intestines breaks down into smaller parts and is absorbed into the blood.

echelon: A formation of people, animals, or vehicles in parallel rows. Each row projects further than the one before it, forming a "V" shape.

germs: Tiny living things that are so small you can't see them. They are everywhere. Some germs can make you sick if they get in your body.

I hope these word definitions are helpful!

DICTIONARY

125

glands: Parts of the body that produce natural chemicals or allow substances to leave the body.

gravity: The force that pulls things down toward Earth.

hibernate: To spend the winter in a deep sleep.

mucus: A slimy fluid that coats and protects the inside of the mouth, nose, and throat.

nectar: A sweet liquid that flowers produce.

nitrogen: A gas that makes up 78 percent of Earth's air. It has no color or odor.

nutrients: Substances that living things need to stay alive. Proteins and vitamins are nutrients.

orbit: The invisible, repeating path followed by an object circling a planet.

oxygen: A gas that humans and animals need to breathe, and fires need to burn. Oxygen makes up 21 percent of Earth's air. It has no color or odor.

peloton: A group of bicyclists riding closely together in a race.

photosynthesis: A process by which green plants make food.

prey: An animal that another animal hunts for food.

protein: A nutrient found in all living plants and animals.

regenerate: To regrow body tissue to replace lost or injured tissue.

rotation: The circular movement of an object around a central point or line.

scientist: Someone who studies the natural and physical world by testing, experimenting, and measuring.

sulfur: A colorless, toxic, flammable gas that is responsible for the foul smell of rotten eggs and farts.

tentacle: A long, flexible limb used by an animal to move, feel, or grasp things.

vitamins: Substances in food that keep people healthy.

water cycle:

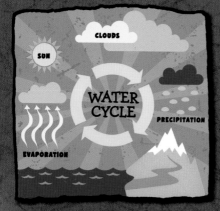

•INDEX•

*Page numbers with an asterisk contain a science project or activity.

IF FLY GUY COULD TALK...

Getting answers to questions is fun and important.

Reporters and police officers know that they always have to answer these six questions.

✓1. Why?
2. What?
3. When?
4. Where?
5. Who?
6. How?

We've done "Why," but we have a lot more questions to answer.

Cool! Let's get started!